FAYETTEVIL

Ecosystems

Oceans

Greg Reid

CHELSEA CLUBHOUSE

An Imprint of Chelsea House Publishers
A Haights Cross Communications Company

Philadelphia

To Mary-Anne, Julian and Damian

This edition first published in 2004 in the United States of America by Chelsea Clubhouse, a division of Chelsea House Publishers and a subsidiary of Haights Cross Communications.

Chelsea Clubhouse
1974 Sproul Road, Suite 400
Broomall, PA 19008-0914

The Chelsea House world wide web address is www.chelseahouse.com

Library of Congress Cataloging-in-Publication Data Applied for.

ISBN 0-7910-7940-6

First published in 2004 by
MACMILLAN EDUCATION AUSTRALIA PTY LTD
627 Chapel Street, South Yarra, Australia, 3141

Associated companies and representatives throughout the world.

Edited by Anna Fern and Miriana Dasovic
Text and cover design by Polar Design
Illustrations and maps by Alan Laver, Shelly Communications
Photo research by Legend Images

Printed in China

Acknowledgments

The author and publisher are grateful to the following for permission to reproduce copyright material:

Cover photograph: a green turtle in the ocean, courtesy of Photodisc.

Norbert Wu/ANTphoto.com.au, pp. 15 (center), 17; François Gohier/Auscape International, p. 15 (bottom); Karen Gowlett-Holmes – OSF/Auscape International, p. 22; Ken Smith Laboratory, Scripps Institute of Oceanography – OSF/Auscape International, p. 16; Mike Langford/Auscape International, p. 20; Wayne Lawler/Auscape, p. 27 (bottom); Mark Spencer/Auscape International, p. 13 (bottom right); Australian Picture Library/Corbis, pp. 15 (top right), 21; Corbis Digital Stock, p. 9 (bottom); Digital Vision, pp. 3 (top), 13 (bottom left), 31; Getty Images/Image Bank, pp. 14, 15 (top left); Getty Images/Photographer's Choice, p. 6; Wade Hughes/Lochman Transparencies, p. 24; G. Saueracker/Lochman Transparencies, p. 18; Alex Steffe/Lochman Transparencies, p. 10; Geoff Taylor/Lochman Transparencies, pp. 9 (top), 13 (top right); NOAA, p. 27 (top); Photodisc, pp. 3 (center & bottom), 5 (top), 7, 11 (top), 12, 13 (center), 23, 25, 26, 29, 30 (both), 32; Photolibrary.com/SPL, pp. 13 (top left), 19; Reuters, p. 28.

While every care has been taken to trace and acknowledge copyright, the publisher tenders their apologies for any accidental infringement where copyright has proved untraceable. Where the attempt has been unsuccessful, the publisher welcomes information that would redress the situation.

Please note
At the time of printing, the Internet addresses appearing in this book were correct. Owing to the dynamic nature of the Internet, however, we cannot guarantee that all these addresses will remain correct.

The author would like to thank Anatta Abrahams, Janine Hanna, Eulalie O'Keefe, Kerry Regan, Marcia Reid.

Contents

When a word is printed in **bold**, you can look up its meaning in the Glossary on page 31.

What Are Oceans?

Oceans are large areas of salt water that are full of life. They wash the shores of all the continents and fill huge holes in the land. From space, Earth looks blue because of the oceans. They cover about 71 percent of Earth's surface at an average depth of 2.4 miles (3.8 kilometers).

An ocean environment is part of an ecosystem. An ecosystem is made up of living plants and animals and their non-living environment of air, water, energy, and nutrients.

Oceans contain 97 percent of Earth's water. They are home to millions of plant and animal **species**, including fish, sea **mammals**, reptiles, seabirds, shellfish, seaweeds, and other **marine** life. Nearly half of all animal species on Earth live in oceans.

Oceans, seas, and continents of the world

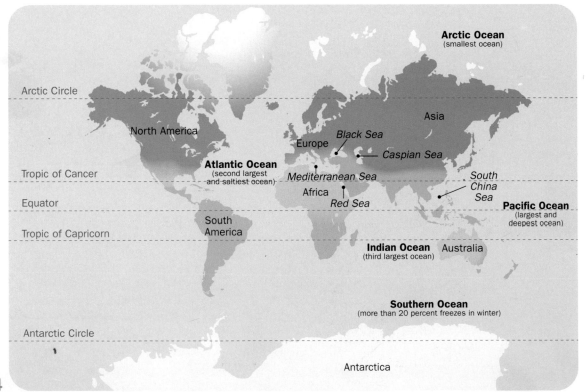

Arctic Ocean
(smallest ocean)

Arctic Circle

Asia

North America

Europe | Black Sea

Caspian Sea

Tropic of Cancer

Atlantic Ocean
(second largest
and saltiest ocean)

Mediterranean Sea

South
China
Sea

Africa

Red Sea

Equator

Pacific Ocean
(largest and
deepest ocean)

Tropic of Capricorn

South
America

Indian Ocean Australia
(third largest ocean)

Southern Ocean
(more than 20 percent freezes in winter)

Antarctic Circle

Antarctica

What Are Oceans Like?

Oceans may be large or small, warm or cold, deep or shallow. The Pacific Ocean is the largest and deepest of the five oceans. It covers about one-third of Earth's surface. Some oceans are saltier than others. The Atlantic Ocean is the saltiest ocean.

In winter, the Arctic Ocean is covered by ice, and more than 20 percent of the Southern Ocean is frozen. In summer, the ice melts and huge icebergs float in the oceans.

The bottom of the ocean has volcanic mountains called seamounts, deep valleys called trenches, and wide, flat plains. Many of these features are larger than those on the land. The deepest part of any ocean is the Mariana Trench. It is 36,204 feet (11,035 meters) deep, and is found in the Pacific Ocean.

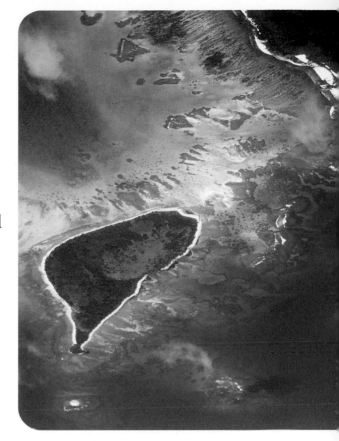

The Pacific Ocean is home to some of the most beautiful islands in the world.

Ocean sizes

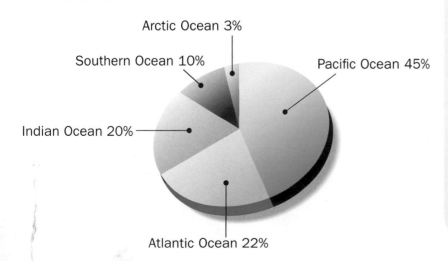

Arctic Ocean 3%

Southern Ocean 10%

Pacific Ocean 45%

Indian Ocean 20%

Atlantic Ocean 22%

Small Oceans

Seas are smaller areas of oceans that are partly enclosed by land. The saltiest sea is the Red Sea. The largest sea is the South China Sea. The Mediterranean Sea is mostly surrounded by land. Some large inland lakes, such as the Caspian Sea and the Black Sea in Asia, have also been called seas.

Waves and Tides

The surface of the oceans is never still. Waves are made by winds that blow over the ocean and can travel long distances from where they are formed. Sometimes, during hurricanes, huge waves called storm surges develop. Waves are usually small during calm periods.

Tides are the regular rise and fall of the level of the oceans. They are caused by the pull of the Moon and the Sun. When the Moon and the Sun are in line, the large tides are called spring tides. When the Moon and the Sun are at right angles to each other, the smaller tides are called neap tides. Some oceans have large tides up to 49.5 feet (15 meters), while other places, such as the Mediterranean Sea, have very small tides.

Waves are caused by winds.

Ecofact

Killer Waves

Tsunamis are waves caused by undersea earthquakes, volcanoes, or landslides. They are usually 3 feet (1 meter) high at sea and travel up to 500 miles (800 kilometers) an hour. Near the coast they may reach up to 130 feet (40 meters) high and cause great destruction.

Currents

Ocean water moves in large circles and swirls, called currents. Currents are the super-highways of the oceans, moving water and nutrients around. There are many different currents. One large current, called the Gulf Stream, moves water from the Caribbean Sea across the Atlantic Ocean and into northern Europe. The Gulf Stream carries more water than all the rivers on Earth.

Currents mainly flow between 1 and 2 miles (1.5 and 3 kilometers) an hour. They are warm near the Equator and cold near the polar regions. Currents get their energy from winds, which, in turn, get their energy from the Sun. Winds drive currents from the Equator to the poles and from the poles to the Equator. Oceans are always moving with waves, tides, and currents.

Ecofact

Ocean Travelers

Many tiny organisms, such as **plankton**, and some larger animals, such as Portuguese man-of-war jellyfish, drift around the oceans carried by currents. They can hardly move through the water on their own, so they depend on currents to move about.

Jellyfish are carried around by ocean currents.

Ocean Zones

Oceans have six zones of life. Each zone has different animals adapted to the conditions of that zone. These conditions include the amount of sunlight, the movement of water, the water temperature, salinity, and **water pressure**.

Ocean zones

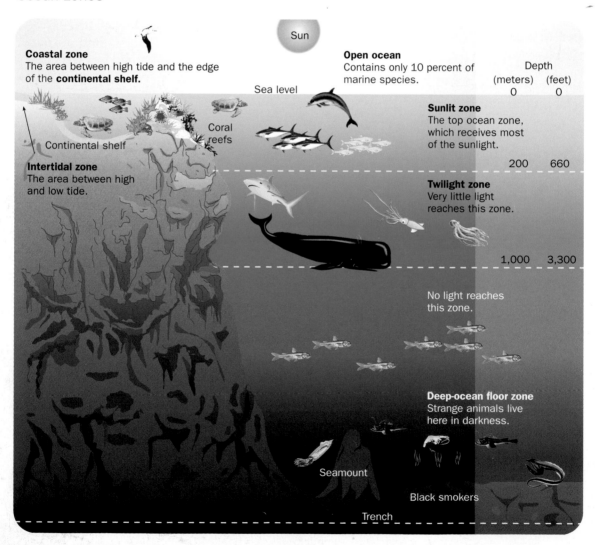

Coastal zone
The area between high tide and the edge of the **continental shelf.**

Sun

Open ocean
Contains only 10 percent of marine species.

Sea level

Coral reefs

Continental shelf

Intertidal zone
The area between high and low tide.

Depth	
(meters)	(feet)
0	0

Sunlit zone
The top ocean zone, which receives most of the sunlight.

200	660

Twilight zone
Very little light reaches this zone.

1,000	3,300

No light reaches this zone.

Deep-ocean floor zone
Strange animals live here in darkness.

Seamount

Black smokers

Trench

Food Chains

In each zone of the ocean there are **food chains**, which show the feeding relationship between plants and animals. A food chain starts with the Sun and nutrients from seawater. These basic elements supply energy for tiny plants called **phytoplankton**. These plants, such as yellow-green algae, drift near the ocean surface. The next link in the chain occurs when animal plankton, called **zooplankton**, eat these tiny plants. Zooplankton are the smallest animals in the food chain. They include the **larvae** of shrimp and fish.

Small fish, such as sardines, eat the zooplankton. In turn, the sardines are eaten by larger fish, such as cod. The food chain ends at the top predator, such as a shark or a killer whale. When any plant or animal in the chain dies, **scavengers**, such as crabs, and **decomposers**, such as worms and bacteria, break down the matter. The decomposed material returns to the seawater, where phytoplankton take up the nutrients to grow, and the cycle continues.

Killer whales are at the top of the food chain in parts of the Pacific Ocean.

Giant Sharks

The largest sharks are harmless plankton feeders. Whale sharks live in tropical oceans and grow to 45 feet (13.7 meters). They filter phytoplankton and zooplankton with their huge mouths.

The whale shark is the world's largest fish.

Coastal Zone

The coastal zone starts at the high-tide mark and finishes at the edge of the continental shelf. The coastal zone has warmer and shallower water than the open ocean. It also contains more nutrients, because rivers flush nutrients from the land into the ocean. The coastal zone occupies only 10 percent of oceans, but it contains 90 percent of all marine species.

Estuaries and coral reefs are two important ecosystems in the coastal zone. Estuaries are where rivers meet the ocean. They are breeding grounds for many animals, such as fish, shrimps, and crabs.

Tiny animals called coral polyps build coral reefs. Coral reefs cover only about 0.17 percent of ocean floors, but they contain more than 25 percent of all marine species. The coastal zone is very small, but it is very rich in marine life.

Ecofact

Ocean Fish

There are about 13,300 species of fish living in the oceans, including about 250 species of sharks. They range from the smallest fish, a 0.4-inch-long (1-centimeter-long) Indian Ocean goby, to the largest fish, the whale shark, which grows to 45 feet (13.7 meters).

Coral reefs swarm with marine life.

Intertidal Zone

The intertidal zone is at the edge of the coastal zone. Different animals live in the four parts of this zone. They have adapted to being exposed to the air between the high and low tides.

The intertidal zone for rocky coasts is different from that in sandy or muddy coasts. Animals on rocky coasts are easier to see, especially in tidal pools. Some animals, such as periwinkles, move about looking for food. Others, such as sea anemones, stay in the same place and filter the water for their food. On sandy and muddy coasts, most animals, such as worms and shellfish, are harder to see because they live under the sand or mud.

Burrowing Animals

Animals, such as cockleshells, blood worms, and pipis, burrow into the middle-tide area of sandy and muddy coasts to feed and hide from predators. In the low-tide area, animals, such as sand dollars and brittle stars, live underground.

Sand dollars are related to starfish. They can be found in the sand at low tide.

Intertidal zone on a rocky coast

Splash area
Some lichens and periwinkles

Sun

Highest high tide

High-tide area

limpets, chitons, periwinkles, green algae, sea anemones — Lowest high tide

Rock pools at low tide

Middle-tide area
barnacles, mussels, oysters, red algae, hermit crabs

Highest low tide

Low-tide area
sea urchins, starfish, tube worms, red algae, swimming crabs

Lowest low tide

Sunlit Zone

The sunlit zone is the top 660 feet (200 meters) of the open ocean. Here, there is a lot of sunlight, and the water is warmer than in the deeper zones. Currents also move the water around in this zone. Ocean plants, such as kelp, grow in the sunlit zone and provide food and shelter for animals.

The sunlit zone is home to many living things, including:

- fish, such as sunfish, tuna, and marlin
- sea mammals, such as whales, dolphins, and seals
- birds, such as albatrosses, petrels, and terns
- other marine life, such as plankton and jellyfish.

Animals move around either by swimming or by floating with the currents. They live alone or in groups, such as schools of fish or pods of whales. The sunlit zone has many animals that move around the oceans of the world.

A school of barracuda in the sunlit zone

Sunlit Zone Food Chain

In the sunlit zone, there are many plants and animals connected in food chains. Here is an example of a food chain from the sunlit zone.

Phytoplankton get their energy from the Sun, and nutrients from the water.

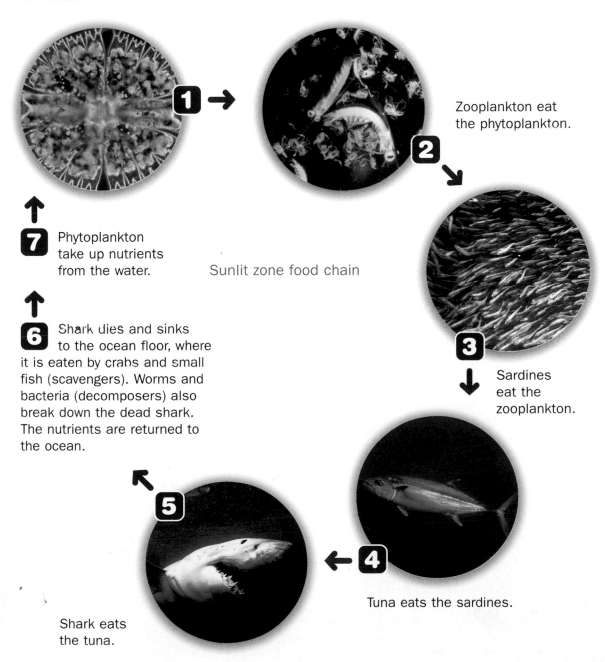

Zooplankton eat the phytoplankton.

Phytoplankton take up nutrients from the water.

Sunlit zone food chain

Shark dies and sinks to the ocean floor, where it is eaten by crabs and small fish (scavengers). Worms and bacteria (decomposers) also break down the dead shark. The nutrients are returned to the ocean.

Sardines eat the zooplankton.

Tuna eats the sardines.

Shark eats the tuna.

Twilight Zone

The twilight zone lies below the sunlit zone. It extends from 660 feet (200 meters) to 3,300 feet (1,000 meters) below the ocean surface. This zone is called the twilight zone because only blue light, which is similar to the light at dawn and dusk, reaches these depths. No plants live in the twilight zone because there is not enough light for them to get the energy they need. Water in the twilight zone is colder than in the sunlit zone, and there is more water pressure and less oxygen.

Animals living here and in the deeper zones below depend on food from the sunlit zone to survive. Some animals that live in the twilight zone, such as squid and pearly nautiluses, move up to the sunlit zone at night to feed. Other animals, such as sea cucumbers, eat dead animal and plant matter that sinks down from the upper sunlit layer. This dead matter is called "marine snow" because it looks like falling snow.

Ecofact

Deep Divers

Sperm whales are deep-diving mammals. They can dive down to the bottom of the twilight zone. Sperm whales are the largest of the toothed whales and grow up to 66 feet (20 meters) long. A thick layer of blubber protects them from the cold water.

Squids are very good swimmers.

Twilight Zone Food Chain

There are many animals connected in food chains in the twilight zone. Here is an example of a food chain from the twilight zone.

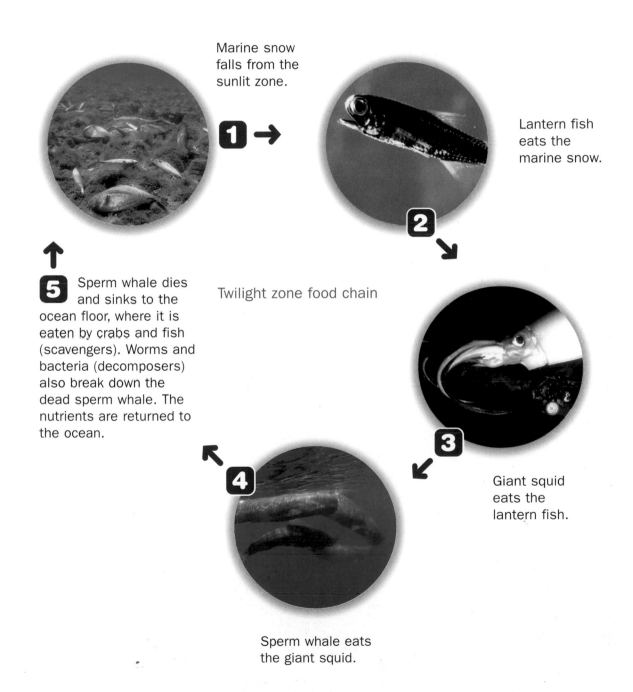

Marine snow falls from the sunlit zone.

1 →

Lantern fish eats the marine snow.

2 ↘

Twilight zone food chain

5 Sperm whale dies and sinks to the ocean floor, where it is eaten by crabs and fish (scavengers). Worms and bacteria (decomposers) also break down the dead sperm whale. The nutrients are returned to the ocean.

3

Giant squid eats the lantern fish.

4

Sperm whale eats the giant squid.

Deep-Ocean Zone

The deep-ocean zone lies below the twilight zone and is in total darkness. It extends below 3,300 feet (1,000 meters) from the ocean surface. Around 85 percent of oceans are more than 3,300 feet (1,000 meters) deep. The deep-ocean zone has colder temperatures and more water pressure than the twilight zone because it is deeper.

Animals living in the deep-ocean zone have many different ways of finding food. Some animals, such as squid, move up to the sunlit zone at night to feed. Other animals, such as viper fish and giant squid, are **predators**, hunting other animals. Animals, such as brittle stars, sea cucumbers, and sponges, feed on marine snow that sinks down from the upper layers. Elephant seals swim from the ocean surface to the deep ocean zone, where they feed on shrimps, squid, and fish.

A sea cucumber (an animal related to starfish) moves across the sea floor at a depth of 13,400 feet (4,100 meters).

Ecofact

Mighty Mouths

Gulper eels live in the deep-ocean zone. They have huge jaws and elastic stomachs so they can eat fish larger than themselves. When they eat a big fish, they do not have to eat for a long time.

Deep-Ocean Animal Adaptations

Animals in the deep-ocean zone have many **adaptations** for survival. Viperfish, deep-sea anglerfish, snake dragonfish, and devilfish have huge mouths and needle-sharp teeth to grip prey. Many fish have strange shapes. Oarfish have long, flattened bodies like eels and long feelers on top of their heads and under their jaws. These feelers may be used to find prey in the darkness.

Deep-sea anglerfish have a lure on top of their head that glows. They use this like a living fishing rod. Shrimp and small deep-ocean fish, such as the hatchetfish, feed on plankton that also produces light. When shrimp and small fish come near the deep-sea anglerfish, they are eaten. Many animals, such as lantern fish, produce light in their bodies to hide or escape from predators, find mates, or look for prey.

A deep-sea anglerfish

Ecofact

Vampire Squid

The vampire squid is one of the best known of the deep-ocean squids. It has sharp spines underneath its tentacles. It lifts its tentacles and the webbing between them up over its body like a cloak to protect itself from predators.

Deep-Ocean Floor Zone

The deep-ocean floor is dark, still, and cold. Because of its great depth, the water pressure on the deep-ocean floor is the greatest of all the zones. The floor is sometimes covered in fine **ooze** that has settled from the top zones.

Animals include sea cucumbers which are 95 percent water, sponges, tubeworms, brittle stars, and shrimps. Most of these animals move slowly.

Animals have many adaptations for survival. Tripod fish have long fins so they can rest on the ocean floor without sinking into the ooze. Sea spiders have long legs so they can move about on the deep-ocean floor. They have no eyes, and they use their long legs to feel for the sponges, sea anemones, and other food that they eat. Scientists believe there are many more species of animals yet to be discovered in the deepest zones of the oceans.

Ecofact

Giant Sea Spider

Most sea spiders that live on the deep-ocean floor are only 0.039 to 0.39 inches (1 to 10 millimeters). However, the colossus sea spider is larger. Its body is longer than 1.9 inches (5 centimeters) and its legs span almost 24 inches (60 centimeters) from one side to the other.

Sea spiders use their legs to find their prey.

Deep-Sea Vents

Deep-sea vents are cracks in the deep-ocean floor made by hot liquid rock, called lava, deep in the Earth's crust. Water in the cracks is heated to more than 760 degrees Fahrenheit (404 degrees Celsius). It dissolves minerals, such as sulfur, and flows out like black jets. Deep-sea vents often have chimneys, called "black smokers," which are made from deposits of the dissolved minerals.

Deep-sea vents are rich in life compared with the rest of the deep-ocean floor. Heat-loving bacteria use the sulfur around deep-sea vents for food. The bacteria provide food for other animals in deep-sea food chains. Giant bright-red tubeworms more than 10 feet (3 meters) long, and giant white clams have the bacteria living inside them. This is called **symbiosis**. Both organisms help each other to survive. There are many more animal species yet to be discovered around deep-sea vents.

Ecofact

Undersea Oases

Deep-sea vents have as much life per square foot as tropical rain forests. Animals, such as white vent crabs and eyeless shrimps, have adapted to the extreme heat within a few feet of the vents and the extreme cold a little further away from the vents.

A black smoker deep-sea vent, several miles beneath the surface of the Atlantic Ocean

Indigenous Peoples

Many **indigenous peoples** live in coastal areas and on islands around the world. These people use the oceans as a food supply. They fish and hunt mammals, such as dugong and seals, and reptiles, such as turtles. In Asia, some people use fishing birds called cormorants to dive down and catch fish for them. Indigenous people also gather plants, such as seaweed, and shellfish, such as oysters, to eat.

Indigenous peoples use a variety of boats to travel around the oceans. In the Pacific Ocean, the Melanesian peoples of New Guinea and nearby islands use outrigger canoes. These are hollowed-out logs with floating arms on one side to keep the canoes stable. The Inuits, who live in the Arctic, have canoes made from animal bones and skins because there are no trees where they live.

Ecofact

Diving for Sea Slugs

In some tropical oceans, indigenous people dive down to the ocean floor looking for sea slugs called trepang. Sea slugs are dried and sold to people in Asia who eat them.

In China, cormorants are used to catch fish.

Living by the Ocean

Indigenous peoples have many different ways of living near the ocean. The Inuits make igloos from blocks of ice. They hunt polar bears, walruses, and seals, and fish through holes in the ice when the Arctic Ocean is frozen. Because it is so cold, Inuits wear thick fur clothes made from the skins of animals they hunt.

In Southeast Asia, the Bajau live as sea **nomads** across a group of islands covering more than 4,000 miles (6,500 kilometers). They live in houseboats called *lepas* and in villages built on stilts over the water. The Bajau trade in sea slugs and move about looking for fish to eat and to sell.

Some Bajau live in stilt villages over the sea in the Philippines, Indonesia, and Malaysia.

Living on the Water

Some Bajau live in houseboats in groups of two to six families. The 35-foot-long (10-meter-long) and 7-foot-wide (2-meter) houseboats have a roof made of mats which are held up with poles. There is a cooking area where all meals are made. Sometimes several boats are joined together by small bridges.

Ocean Resources

Oceans are a source of food for many people. Harvesting wild fish, shrimp, crabs, crayfish, shellfish, and other species is a large industry in many countries. People across the world eat more seafood than beef and chicken.

Fish farming is also important, with more than 4.4 million tons (4 million metric tons) of fish produced a year. About 25 percent of the world's total seafood production now comes from fish farms. Seahorses, seaweed, shrimp, and shellfish, such as oysters, are also farmed.

Scientists are planning to harvest tiny shrimp called krill that live in the Southern Ocean. Krill could be used as stock feed, pet food, and for humans to eat. Krill are the main food source of many animals, such as whales. People must be careful not to take too much from the oceans, or the food chains will be disturbed and there will be little seafood left in the future.

Sorting a catch of squid on board a southern Australian fishing boat

Minerals, Energy, and Chemicals

Oceans have rich deposits of minerals, oil, and natural gas. Nearly a quarter of the world's supply of oil and natural gas comes from offshore drilling rigs. Gold, diamonds, tin, and titanium are mined on some coastal areas. In some places on the deep-ocean floor, there are round lumps of manganese, copper, nickel, and cobalt. These resources may be mined in the future.

Oceans are also a source of energy. Electricity can be made by using the energy of the tides and the waves. This causes no pollution, and the energy is renewable.

Oceans have many organisms with useful chemicals that help people. Drugs to help fight cancer have come from some sponges. A strong sunscreen chemical has been found in some corals. Oceans have many resources to help people, but we must use them wisely.

Ecofact

Mining Seawater

Seawater has been used for thousands of years to make salt. In recent times, about 13,000 factories around the world are turning seawater into freshwater. Desert countries by the sea are very interested in this.

An offshore oil-drilling platform

Threats to Oceans

Over-fishing is one of the biggest threats to oceans. People are using bigger ships and nets, as well as technology, such as sonar and spotter planes, to find and catch larger schools of fish. Some whales and fish species, such as southern bluefin tuna, are **endangered** because too many have been caught.

There may not be enough fish left to breed unless we control how many we catch. Scientists say that 70 percent of the major fish species that are caught, such as cod and haddock, are in danger of being over-fished. Over-fishing may lead to the extinction of some species. Fishing needs to be carefully managed so valuable fish resources continue to be used into the future.

Ecofact

Fishing Victims

Up to 40 percent of the animals caught in fishing nets, drift nets, and long fishing lines in the oceans are wasted by being thrown out after they are dead. Seabirds, dugongs, dolphins, turtles, small fish, and sharks are often killed in this way. These unwanted animals are called bycatch.

Because of over-fishing, the number of southern bluefin tuna has been reduced to about 2 to 5 percent of the original population.

Ocean Pollution

Pollution is a major threat to oceans. For many years, people have dumped waste into the oceans, including radioactive material. Sewage pumped into oceans causes poisonous algae to grow. Litter, such as plastic bags and other garbage, can float in the oceans and be swallowed by animals, or caught around them. Rivers wash industrial chemicals, fertilizers, and pesticides from the land and into the oceans, where they affect sea life.

Oil spills float on the surface of the ocean. The oil harms animals by choking them and coating their fur or feathers. Many animals are killed from oil spills. Ocean pollution damages sea animals and their food chains. We need to clean up our oceans and stop the pollution.

Ecofact

Deadly Poison

Inuits live in one of the cleanest areas of the world. Yet the seals and other animals they eat have some DDT pesticide in their bodies. Although DDT has not been widely used for 20 years, it is still found in air and water around the world.

Dead sea birds and rubbish are collected in the aftermath of an oil spill.

Effects of Human Activities on Oceans

Humans are changing the climate by burning fuels, such as coal and oil. This increases the amount of carbon dioxide in the air and adds to **global warming**. As a result, polar ice caps and glaciers could melt and the level of the oceans could rise. Global warming would also change the winds and the pattern of ocean currents. Coral reef ecosystems would also be changed.

Rising sea levels would flood some low-lying coastal areas and island nations, such as the Maldives in the Indian Ocean. Many millions of people around the world would lose their homes. People would need to move or build expensive sea walls for protection. Human actions are having an effect on the oceans and they will have further effects on us.

Ecofact

Sea Walls

The Netherlands already has long sea walls to protect parts of the country that are lower than the level of the sea. If sea levels rise, these walls will need to be made higher and longer or the land will be flooded.

Rising sea levels would drown islands, such as this one in the Pacific Ocean.

Foreign Invaders and Pollution

Cargo ships traveling around the world carry seawater in their ballast tanks to keep them stable. When this water is released, any foreign organisms in that water are deposited into the ocean. These foreign species, such as zebra mussels, can destroy the local sea life and upset the ecosystem. Scientists say that around 3,000 marine species travel in ship ballast tanks every day. More efforts are needed to control the release of ballast water so foreign species do not invade other ecosystems.

Ocean pollution affects the health of marine animals and the people who eat them. Seafood, especially shellfish, can easily become contaminated with pollution. Bacteria from sewage can also cause diseases, such as cholera. The oceans need to be protected from pollution or everyone suffers.

Coral Reef Danger

Pollution, over-fishing, and global warming have destroyed more than 25 percent of coral reefs. Warmer water temperatures from global warming are causing many corals to die. This is called coral bleaching.

These are the white skeletons of corals killed by warmer water temperatures and pollution.

Sewage released into oceans is a threat because it contains bacteria that can cause diseases.

Protecting Oceans

More laws are needed to protect oceans and stop over-fishing. Some countries have set limits on the amount of fish that can be caught, and only allow fishing at certain times of the year. This gives the fish time to recover and increase their numbers. However, in **international waters**, there are few laws, and fish continue to be taken in large numbers.

International laws have been made for dumping dangerous waste, such as plastics and radioactive material, in oceans. These are very dangerous because they take a long time to break down and they are a threat to animals and people. Oil tankers are no longer allowed to clean their tanks in international waters. People and governments around the world need to be aware of the threats to oceans, and take actions to protect them.

This Russian fishing vessel was caught illegally driftnetting off the coast of Alaska.

Marine Parks and Reserves

Marine parks and reserves protect only small areas of oceans. The largest marine park is the Great Barrier Reef Marine Park, in Australia. It is also the largest coral reef and covers an area of 134,634 square miles (348,700 square kilometers). The Great Barrier Reef contains a large variety of species found nowhere else in the world. There are around 2,000 fish species, 500 coral species, more than 400 sponge species, and 11 species of sea snakes. The Great Barrier Reef is a major tourist attraction.

A large whale sanctuary in the Southern Ocean now protects more than 90 percent of the world's whale population. However, Japan and Norway do not recognize the sanctuary and continue to hunt whales there. Governments need to do more to protect the oceans and marine life.

The green turtle is protected, but it is still hunted illegally.

Protected Species

Some endangered species, such as green turtles, are protected. International agreements have been made to stop the illegal trade in endangered animals. However, green turtles are still hunted in some countries, such as Indonesia and Mexico.

How to Save Oceans

We can all work to save oceans. You can learn more about the importance of oceans to the world. Join a conservation group, such as Greenpeace, and let others know about the threats to oceans. Do not leave garbage on the beach or put oil down the sink.

Report ocean pollution to the proper authorities. Write to the government and ask them to help save the world's oceans. The governments of rich countries can help poor countries protect their oceans for the good of everyone.

ecosystems

The following web sites give more information on oceans.

Aquatic environments
http://curriculum.calstatela.edu/courses/builders/lessons/less/biomes/aquatic.html

Earth's oceans
http://www.enchantedlearning.com/subjects/ocean/index.shtml

Marine ecosystems
http://mbgnet.mobot.org/salt/

OceanLink
http://www.oceanlink.island.net/main.html

Oceans Alive
http://www.abc.net.au/oceans/alive.htm

Oceans on line
http://www.oceansonline.com/lib_bio_ocean.htm

Glossary

adaptations	changes that help plants and animals survive in an environment
continental shelf	the shallow coastal area surrounding continents
decomposers	organisms, such as worms, fungi, and bacteria, that break down plant and animal matter
endangered	in danger of becoming extinct
extinction	when no more of a particular species of plant or animal are left on Earth
food chains	a way of showing how plants and animals in an ecosystem depend on each other for food
global warming	the increase in the average temperature of the world
indigenous peoples	groups of people who first lived in a place, whose traditional ways help them to survive in that place
international waters	waters outside the national fishing zones of countries
larvae	the early form of an animal before it becomes an adult
mammals	a group of animals that have hair or fur, warm blood, a large brain, and feed their young milk
marine	having to do with the sea
nomads	people who move from place to place instead of living in one spot
ooze	fine mud and clay that has settled on the ocean floor
phytoplankton	tiny plant-like organisms that drift near the surface of the ocean
plankton	tiny plants and animals that drift around in water
predators	animals that hunt and eat other animals
prey	animals that are hunted and eaten by predators
scavengers	animals that live off dead animals
species	types of plants and animals
symbiosis	when two organisms live together and benefit from each other
water pressure	the force of the weight of water on an object
zooplankton	tiny animal plankton that feed on phytoplankton

Index